AF576835

Falling Season

Tori Lane

Copyright

Omega Publications, Palm Springs, CA

ISBN: 978-0-9850350-3-7

Cover Art by Tori Lane
Cover Design and Layout by Cori Canady
Author Photo by Brodie Pearson

Omega Publications
www.OmegaPublications.net

Printed in the United States of America

Dedication

For Lisa,
    my best elephant,

and for my Khulumani family,
    the strength of my voice.

Falling Season

Contents

Prologue

I am here to find my voice –
not what tentatively whispers,
but that which commands, yells,
cackles aloud, unashamed of its emboldened presence.
Stripping myself of colorful, painted presentation,
letting the voice emerge from within,
the voice long muffled, smothered,
ignored into near non-existence.

I am here to let it rumble –
let it shake loose its chains,
beat on the door and bars of its cell,
trade an inmate's soiled rags for the solid clothes of freedom
and walk blinking, barefoot into startling sun.

I am here to let it holler from atop a mountain,
echoing into thousands of crevices below,
shaking loose the very rocks it climbed.

I am here to let it beat drums next to a midnight fire
and the upward cascade of flashing lights,
let it shout and freely dance in response.

I am here not to seek out a voice
but unleash what has been bound,
expose the voice long hidden,
give it space, make it wings, watch it fly,
or explode in the glory of a beautiful, fiery mistake.

Highway to Buxton

The road, lined with violet sky and water,
moved toward February's rim
where a mobile of shining stars hung in the black
over the black that waved playfully back at them.
The road came to this edge
where the first colors of day murmur over the water
and the sun rumbles into view without a smile,
instead staring with a wide eyed compassion
on this yawning piece of earth.
This is a place with the kind of morning
that is ever giving birth to art, to hope, to faith.
It renews with the subtlety of glory rising into cold, empty air.
It moves over the waves and strolls on the beach,
leaving not footprints, but sweetly warmed winter sand.
This is the kind of morning that gives birth to a writer,
emboldening some quietly articulate piece of spirit
to compose lyrics to the music of the water
that exists only in this moment,
that will never be breathed in or heard quite like this again.

Meeting History

The walls are streaked with mimicries of Northern Lights
as the slowly dipping sun presses
stained glass color into the sanctuary.
Pews flicker with speckled flashes
and worn carpeted aisles glow with muted warmth.
Removing shoes in sacred silence, she treads on the history
of altar calls, invocations, weddings and funerals.
Her skin dances with the honesty of colored light as she slows,
abiding deeply in the silence,
silence thick with the mosaic of memories,
of history developing toward some unfolding infinite.
And there she carves a question in time,
one of faith and the reality of God, joining
the inquiring community that had walked the aisles
and sat in the pews.
She resides with those who have courageously
engaged the questions, bathing in the honesty of colored light
over the years of rising days and falling nights, and there,
in barefooted silence,
she senses a closeness of family
and the nearness of God.

Fusion

It's about breathing.
Finding the breath and tempo of the words.
Letting their rhythm guide inflection, emphasis.
Pause.
The life of language resides inside me
but requires the mystic strength of breath to embolden it to move,
outward from spirit and mind,
across unholy lips to rejoin the open air.
To write is to dance across a page and through space.
Briefly harness a power of creative divinity
and breathe deeply of an unknowable language.
To encounter a greater depth of union
with the Divine who used Word to create.

It's about breathing.
Feeling the pull of movement on limbs.
Breathing deeply and sensing the rhythmic pulse
that forms the beat to every step.
It resides in the flow of blood, the tension of muscles
and needs only attentiveness to freedom to be unleashed.
To dance is to write poetry across a stage with a stylus of feet.
Participate in a duet of Spirit and spirit
that is played out in the richness of tangible expression.
To revel in the unified fullness of intellect, body and spirit
and that wholeness of self connecting with the Divine.

It's about breathing.
Granting attention to the rhythm of inhale, exhale, heartbeat,
and unleashing all restraint,
to move in it.
Write through it.

FALLING SEASON

Abide in the rhythm of body and language.
Engage the fullness of self.
Breathe in unified pace with God.

Late Morning Walk

The little blonde runs ahead of her mom on the sidewalk,
slightly too big toddler jeans hanging on her diaper,
pink sneakered feet moving almost faster than she can handle.

Her mom laughs to herself,
noticing how the corners of strangers' mouths
inevitably reach skyward
when her daughter giggles by.

She bounces up to a pot of flowers outside a store
and with greedy innocence plucks a few,
little ungentle hands squishing petals,
mangling the delicate blooms.

Kneeling beside her,
her mom carefully takes one
and tucks it into the mess of baby blonde hair.
Spinning the little girl around,
she gestures to their reflection in the store window.

Little blue eyes scan the glass until they settle on her mom's gaze.
She smiles as motherly arms envelop her.

Nuzzling her, the smiling mom
whispers into her daughter's ear
and the little one erupts in tickled laughter,
wiggling until she's released.
Her mom remains kneeling,
loving eyes chasing her daughter down the sidewalk.

Quickly, the little girl stops and rushes back

to press a mangled flower into one of her mom's hands and take the other with hers.

The Extra

The day smelled of poetry from its onset,
        though I don’t really know what that means.

It was an undertone in my coffee,
the coffee I drank out of my orange mug
that probably needs a more thorough cleaning
than the rinsing it’s gotten the past three mornings.
It was in the voice of the cat
who was either wishing me a *good morning*
or informing me of the rudeness of my inattention.
It unfolded with my banana peel and
plopped gleefully into my cereal with the milk.
It was the inaudible serenade of the day in the shower
which I sensed only in the breaths between my off key howlings.
It was woven into the red plaid pajama bottoms
and in the skinny black jeans I traded them for.
It was laced with the laces of the chucks
I decided not to wear and
slid into the sandals I did.
It was stamped on my metro card and with me
waiting for the nondescript white walking man
to tell me it’s safe to cross the street.
It was in the backbeat of the songs on my iPod,
the ones changing my pace and
tempting my hips to swagger more in stride.
It was the five dollar ticket to a reading,
the one proposing I pick up my pen and
write down the flash of an idea that led
to this poem being written.

FALLING SEASON

It was in introductions, handshakes, discussions,
laughter, hugs and goodbyes.
It's been in the simple, ordinary dailyness,
down to the last sip of wine in my glass
and the pen writing in my juice stained notebook.

It seems to be the often unrecognized extra tacked onto my ordinary

.

Arms of the Oak

Last summer she tied a dozen ropes
to the arms of the oak in the backyard,
each looped into a noose at the end.
They murmured and swayed each day
in the Virginia summer breeze,
swirled with the painted leaves of falling autumn,
and now cast long dripping shadows over melting February snow.

In the heated summer air,
she would perch in the crevices of the oak arms,
rubbing tanned hands over the bark in the hope of splinters,
kicking well worn sneakers at the dangling ropes,
making them dance in fading sun.
She stared up at the lines and loops
of rope from piles of crunchy colors
as the air began to scorn its own warmth,
trading it for the chill of a more attentively thankful season.
With mushy snow puddling around her feet,
she crouched at the base,
looking into the rope adorned arms of the oak,
wondering if they would finally concede to bend low to the ground,
wrap themselves around her, hold her close the way nightmares do.
She is now settled into the grounded shadow beneath the oak,
watching the steady drips of melting cold fall from the arms.
From the strong arms of the oak, she, too, has hung and fallen,
from the dirty ivory hands at the end of her adorned arms
and from the strangled, unbroken neck of her dreams.

Red Painted Centuries

This night sky settles to rust red – sick, muted red
hovering over slick black streets
illuminated by shops and streetlights.
It's the forever red –

the pulsing color of the clock
echoed in previous centuries.

Centuries bloodstained with battlefields and virgin sheets.
Red painted centuries of adorned crowns and jeweled
robes. Red screams – delivering
mothers, first cried breath.
Red protection painted on doorframes and
salvation flowing from pierced hands and feet.

Wingless

Holding a green teapot, she sits in the silent
patience of her unmoving wings –
little kitchen angel figurine:

unmarked by stains, unfallen, proud
with her wings upheld. Like

the birds proclaiming sunshine
outside my shaded window, she
almost dares to take flight. And I,

in my rumpled plaid pajamas,
curl winglessly around a cup
of peach tea. Hiding under
my quilted spills and stains,

my slouching shadowed spine, bare back
where wings have never been.

The Curve of Questions

Staring out of windows at the day unengaged,
in bed until noon, rolling through uncertainties.
It's a grave stillness with internal wandering,
a day of questions and subtle crisis.
Of faith, unsure of standing, believing,
trusting enough to be still and known.
The heart with a violent quivering beat
punches holes under the curve of questions,
pressing into the trauma of engaged crisis,
the lack of assurance dragged into view
by the ball of light that brings exposure of doubts
and anger not quite openly vented,
mourning not dared to be ventured into.
Cradled in doubting fears, curled into the curve,
putting a gun to the base of the day,
to kiss the knuckle marks of heartbeats,
making threats against the silence.

The Page

The blankness of the page offends the poet –
its void of articulated words
where the pen in hand rebels against
its role as conduit of harnessed divinity.
But an entire world has danced across
the page as the poet has raged
with frustrated curses.
The new sun of morning has spattered
it with memories of history's risen days
that all inevitably crumbled into nights.
The noble movement of air
has swept across it with quietly passing beauty,
murmuring of eternal change.
Fingers have touched it
with swirling crevices, signs of distinction,
impressing unspoken knowledge
of God onto its surface.
The blank page speaks of the future
and it promises nothing
but to receive what dances across it.

Waiting

I feel the thunder rumble in my feet in the windowsill
more than I can hear its quaking.
The pounding rain allows brief respite for my eyes,
sore from crying. The lightning is the only acceptable light,
the only illumination respectful of this waiting,
waiting for the phone call to burst the thick silence,
shatter a season of time by concluding a life,
a call to confirm the end of her breathing
that I know even now is slowing. I try to slow mine
but can't stop the heaves of my crying,
almost trying to compensate for her breath ceasing.
Dear God, I hope she suffers not.
I hope she sees sun and blue sky, hears audible beauty,
holds the hands she's held for sixty loving years.
I'll keep this miserable storm here,
take it into my body with early mourning,
I'll take it in as I learn the depths of missing her,
the start of severe regrets and wishes,
but mainly just missing her.
Even all the colorful fucks and flairs of language
cannot reign in this grieving, an alarm has gone off,
so loud with mourning, no snooze or off button,
only the resounding promise of slightly emptier days
and unending potential for loud regrets.
This exhausted wakefulness came too early, unwelcome,
and I am unprepared in every way to hold this storm of grief
in my tightening chest, in the nausea squeezing my middle,
in the breath that thins to gasps
as I grasp for things I'll probably never hold again.

In Loving Memory of Sue Lane
September 4, 1932 – July 13, 2011

September 4th

Today is her birthday.
She would've been 79 and coming to visit soon.
She would've loved this place,
seeing where I've come to abide and call home,
understanding it more deeply than most others.
I hate that she won't be spending this Fall
adventuring across the East Coast,
seeing the many leaves of New England,
tasting the change of my Northern Virginia seasons.
There were so many plans made for this next year,
but as Grandpa said, It looks like she won't be making it.
I know she would've loved it.
I hate that I'll never get another phone call before I leave on a trip,
no more of that melodic voice on the phone,
no more knowledge of her prayers as I venture into new things.
She exuded something, a presentness
of which I am still only barely aware.
She taught me it long before I was ready to receive such wisdom,
in the way she handled a sudden house full
of her five children, us innumerable grandkids
and the miscellaneous cousins who floated in and out.
She still sat to play with my quiet misfitted self,
not stressed at all, just preciously with me.
I wish she were here with me.
I wish she'd gotten to meet the guy sitting across from me,
whatever actually happens or doesn't between us,
I know she would've liked him.
I wish she, just once, could've seen me dance,
heard me read this poetry,
known the me I've finally been becoming,
present in my own skin as she'd always been in hers.

FALLING SEASON

I wish I could've held her in one more hug,
smelled the shampoo on her white curls,
heard that voice say, I love you and will see you next time.
I wish the seeing her again was true,
that I'd said I love you at least one more time.
Today I'll just say, Happy Birthday, to a cloudless sky,
write, I love you, with remembering tears
and keep quietly wishing for what won't be coming true.

In Loving Memory of Sue Lane
September 4, 1932 – July 13, 2011

TORI LANE

Five O'clock Storm

The storm woke her up three hours early,
in the five o'clock hour of a Sunday,
curled around pillows and under sheets,
listening with fear and awe laced breathing
to how the summer night could rage.
It foretold of nights whimpering with grief,
laying on hardwood floors under open windows,
whispering smoke into humid midnights,
nights when her eyes would empty of their color, the blue and grey
following gravity's pull to smile darkly under new vacancies.
The scream of that storm, having awoken senses to taste
unrivaled grief, echoed through the heated months,
carving paths for her dark explorations.
It pressed holes into the ground, stretching down into the depths,
creating an unmarked cemetery on the surface of her soul.
Standing graveside, she bled the color from her eyes,
sweated tears in a storm of midday sun,
aware of the distant waking rumble of a five o'clock storm
that had tried to tell her what was coming.

Home

In the beige and white matter of the brain,
I get it,
but it refuses to settle,
sink down the line of my spine,
travel south inside jugular veins,
lodge in the heart,
infect blood that pushes out,
permeate the rest of me.
I don't get it in my socked feet
or in the morning stretch of legs,
in the hollow hunger of stomach
or shower wrinkled fingers,
in the tension of shoulders
or the rise and fall of breathing chest –
only behind the eyes,
tucked away inside the matter
where words are formed,
above the neckline of disconnect
between my head and heart.

Imitations

I don't live totally in a void, in the without of hope,
not hope less, but certainly less than hopeful.
Hope has an air of optimistic expectation and
I expect little, nothing, less than what I'd dream of
if I dreamed much at all. I don't dream for lack of belief.
I believe with no sense of dreaming, no claiming
of promised good. I believe as a statement of spiritual fact
but have less than a fullness of faith.
I believe but need help with my overwhelming lack as well.
I want to be an imitation,
not just a cheap knock off but a realistic mimic,
an accurate representation, a current day presentation,
my own adapted version of those who have known hope.

I want to imitate Abraham,
who hoped against hope, in hope believed,
in full persuasion of God's promise and ability to come through.
I am often fully nothing but confused, fearful, doubting,
not daring to expect fulfillment, all but hopeful,
too often fully fact, lacking dreaming capacity and
far reaching vision of God's promise keeping provision.

I want to imitate Moses,
follow the fire and smoke of freedom through desert
toward promise, raise the staff turned snake turned staff
over water and watch it rip apart, pave the grounding for faith,
rather than perpetually flailing, sputtering for air,
trying to swim across the damn thing alone.
I want to imitate Joshua,

run laps around walls, fully confident that one day they'll fall.

I want to imitate David,
throwing rocks at giants, persuaded of divinely infused strength,
fierce in belief and reckless in faith,
rather than fierce only in doubting,
reckless only in throwing questions as rocks
at the giant of God I am so desperate to know.
I want to be able to strip down to my underwear,
dance crazy before the God
I know, trust, believe in because on some level
I've actually seen him.

I want to imitate Elijah,
up the stakes of challenge with taunting and tubs of water,
call fire from heaven and watch bull burn in response.
Like him, I often run for the hills,
rage with fearful trembling and call death down on myself.
But I'd rather hide in a crevice of Horeb,
there feel the empty wind, earthquake, fire's heat,
and then hear the whisper of my promise keeping God.

I want to be an imitation, full of anticipation,
looking forward to the promised city with foundations
whose designer and creator is God.
I want to know the dreadful longing of hope,
the confident assurance in what is not yet
but is promised by him who is faithful.
I want to watch waters rip apart,
walls crumble, giants fall and bulls burn.
I want to be fully persuaded like Abraham,
or at least persuaded enough to throw rocks, spontaneously dance,
and raise the staff turned snake turned staff high above the waters.

Waves

The beach is almost too cold to handle,
but the day too perfect to go back inside just yet.
Each swell seems to be a steady rising inhale,
and the waves roll in, onto the beach,
a long, slow crashing exhale.
Occasionally the exhale reaches up to nudge my cold,
sanded coated feet,
as if it's trying to get my attention, gently, always gently,
asking, why do you struggle so much
to do this most beautiful and simple of things?
I answer aloud, reassured by the honesty of the question,

I have always had a hard time breathing.
I'm fairly certain I hated that first breath
outside the bubble of my mom,
that my first scream was an admission
that I didn't like feeling like a balloon that wouldn't stay full.
The pain of exhaling was the pain of grieving,
losing what I'd only moments before gained,
like momentary love stories, lifetimes and quickly grieved deaths.
I screamed because I didn't want to live a life full of such losses.

I grew up as an asthmatic kid,
the one sitting out in gym class, wheezing into an inhaler,
slowly and subtly growing in girth as physical activity
shrunk and fled from my life.
I grew out of the asthmatic need for inhaler carrying
but there are days when after some kinds of activity,
I still breathe with that quiet, internal wheeze and rattle
and I'm reminded I have always
struggled with the simplest of things.

I also have a hard time breathing when I see someone
who looks like a someone I once knew,
a someone I knew in ways I shouldn't have,
who knew me in ways I didn't like.
I struggle to breathe in those moments
when I don't remember how old I am, where I am,
I forget most of my lived existence
except that someone I once knew and wish I didn't.

I breathe in shakes when I cry and when I remember too much,
when I remember the trembling breath of counting
until something was over.
I've always had a hard time breathing,
it's just how it's always been,
I say to the steady, rumbling breaths of ocean,
to the white of the long crashing exhale.
The ocean refuses to respond to my confession in any way
other than continuing its beautiful and simple pattern of breathing,
and it makes me sad, a little angry,
watching how easily this breathing comes,
but then an exhale reaches up to nudge my cold,
sand coated feet,
as if promising me to teach me, gently, always gently,
how I, too, can breathe.

Words

"A writer can be at home in novel, story, essay or play; it's the breathing inside a blaze of words that counts." – Cynthia Ozick

These are the pieces that matter, the things to be breathed in,
lost within and pushed back out again –
it's breathing inside the blaze, in the fires of white hot
inspired glory, or frustrated, teeth gnashing fury,
entering deep canyons inspired of life, kissing faces
wrinkled with death and lines of redeemed suicide,
walking on starvation quaking dirt, rubbing fingers through
the hair of a sleeping child, and taking a drink
of undeniable depravities. The words ensnare and equally set free,
slaughtering the uncaptured flight of moments, grounding them
in recording pages beautiful to give them
immortal wings of repetition.
Each word carrying the memory of a thousand tragedies
and near miraculous glories, and, even more momentous,
the subtle, barely noticed imperfections that compose
the life between all extremes. The words blaze hotter, taste sweeter
in those tiny monotonies, in the ways between rights and wrongs,
in all the murmurs of grey, in the ethereal colors of memory
unconsciously claimed. These intangible sounds on tongues,
script curling across pages, pull all things earthy and vulgar,
all heavenly and without stain from physicality into
the sustaining memory of history. Sticks and stones
may fracture bones but these words can bury them alive,
commit them to heavens and flames, force them to commune
at the tables with angels or to bed for the night with demons.
These words can embalm a fleck of time within language,
tame the chaos of a moment and declare it unapologetically divine,
not wicked or good, merely made into epic, doomed to live
in realms beyond its own, to wait for generations yet unified,

still in their pieces in those who will make them whole.
These words carry creation in all its havoc, the ruinations
of silence, the wonders of dying and of breath.
They are the foundations, winding walls and air within a labyrinth,
treaded within slowly, reverently, with fear and obverse awe,
a meditation on realities and illusions, promises of remembrance,
offerings of depths to wander, fires to be consumed by,
unending places to go and air to breathe in slowly
as well as in gasps, laughter and screams.

The Best Valentines

My first boyfriend, long before he was my boyfriend,
surprised me for Valentine's Day with a rose,
handmade card and stuffed panther.
He didn't have his license so his mom
had to drive him the thirty minutes
to my church where I was doing childcare for a banquet.
I stood in unmoving disbelief as he crossed the room
to where I stood picking packing peanuts out of a little girl's hair.

My last boyfriend, the day before he was officially my boyfriend,
asked me to take a study break
a few evenings before Valentine's Day.
He showed up at my door with a duct tape rose he'd made,
a pink and red valentine with a sonnet he'd written
and a heart shaped dish full of carrots,
my favorite study food that last year of college.

The next year, that boyfriend,
who'd by then become my long distance boyfriend,
drove four hours to celebrate our anniversary and Valentine's Day.
He brought me a potted plant with sweet, little, red flowers.
I tried really hard to keep that sweet little plant alive
but within a month all the flowers had turned crispy and fallen off
and it looked like the dead of winter in early spring.

By far, the best Valentine's Day is this year,
stretched out on the couch, icing a rehearsal sore knee
in an empty house.
I got another heart shaped dish from a boy today,
this dish filled with chocolate,
this boy four years old and in my preschool class.

FALLING SEASON

I sit, munching on carrots,
going through valentines with names written in crayon,
heart stickers, a Buzz Lightyear lollipop, a Toy Story pencil,
a butterfly stick-on tattoo and pictures of fairy princesses.
The best Valentine's Day is a martini
and making dinner for one in my sweats,
knowing I am loved with pure, crayon colored,
sticker stuck kinds of love
and having a good reason to wear
a butterfly stick-on tattoo on my hand.

Searching

It's late. Dark outside. I sit in the sliver of my room lit by my laptop screen. The cursor blinks at me from the Google image search bar, waiting. I stare at it. Five. Ten. Thirty minutes. I let my fingers graze the keys in debate.

This is a bad idea. Will lead nowhere good. And it's not what you'd think. Porn. Or something sexual at all. In some twisted corner of my mind it's alluring – but that's not the point.

Blood.

That's the point. Well, the result of a point. Of an edge. Deliciously sharp. Dipping beneath the top layers of skin, willing them to divide and the resulting gap to fill with a rush of red. The opposite of Moses parting waters – this is an entirely unholy act.

I want to search for it, see it. Let the computer's glow be tinted – tainted – red with the posted pictures of those who indulged as I want to. My unknown but best understood friends.

Tapping the keys in rapid succession. C-U-T-T-I-N-G. Auto-complete's first suggestion is *cutting yourself.*

Yes, please.

I delete the word. I shouldn't do it. It's playing with fire. But that's never been as tempting – burning never did have the same effect, the satisfaction of a cut.

I play with my hair up. Pick at my fingernails. Chew on my lip. Biting until there is a taste of blood.

I quickly type again. C-U-T-T-I-N-G. And smash the ENTER key without a second thought.

Pineapples.

Cutting boards and damn pineapples!

I type again. C-U-T-T-I-N-G. And scroll down to auto-complete suggestion one.

First result – someone who accidently cut off a finger tip. No thanks. A little too extreme, even for me.

Second result – SLAYER carved into a forearm. Closer but it's not enough and there are no other good results.

I type again, changing the search.

S-E-L-F, SPACE, I-N-J-U-R-Y.

Much better results! Scarred forearms. Slits oozing blood, reverse sea-parting style. I am envious. Of boldness. Of perceived lack of shame. Regret.

I'd regret it. Over a year without – a damn eternity after going seven years deep into unholy miracles of parting skin to see the rush of red.

I close the search engine with a quivering finger tap.

I still see it. The parting of forearm flesh. Feel the pulling separation of skin. I suck in my lower lip, seeking the vaguely lingering taste. I can almost taste it.

Almost will myself to feel it. All that's left is to do it.

I close my laptop, crawl into bed, fully clothed. Leaving clean up for tomorrow.

Smoked Dry

Smoked me dry at the end of the day,
hidden in a bottle of wine, half drunk,
half buried in hourglass sand,
choking on dehydrated kernels of time.
Autumnal leaves crushed into fine powder,
broke the bottle's neck, carved a heartbeat into my chest,
rubbed in the dust of leaving to mark this fall,
tattooing life's progression onto skin
over the bruises from breathing too deeply,
ribs snapped back to make space for more.
Left trails in the night, of grey and heat,
leading to places of near drunken communions
and bodies taken deep with pains.
Soon only salt water stains will remain,
caked around feet with sand and time.
I may be in need of something to remember you by.

Yes, Thank You

Twenty miles per hour around the curve past my perch,
slow down the pace, give thanks for unwanted breath
and steps so brutal they hurt my heart,
every bit of pressure on the ground, every expansion of lungs,
yes, thank you, God, for this life.
Wailing with solitude, this swagger down empty streets,
I fill them with smoke and touch each low hanging tree limb,
feeling the crevices of weather and time
with each splintering tear drop that mists down from clouds,
daring to cover up the stars for my lonely pleasure.
A soul is raw like the weathered wood of this bench,
tucked leaf crunching steps off the sidewalk.
I watch the cars go by, know there are people inside
but never have I felt so alone on this giving thanks night
when I can wail into silence and no one would know,
no one would hear the sound or register the silence
I'd leave when this breath runs out.

Hand Crafted Box

I would like to crawl out of my skin,
turn around and beat the ever-living hell out of it,
leave it in a pile on the floor.
Then break my fingers and my feet,
use the bones to make a box.
Spit, blood and fingernails
would make putty to fill in the gaps
before I wrap it in the soft red and purpled skin.
I'd cut off all my hair to weave a nest inside
to hold my memories, with an eye for a pillow
and a heavy blanket of my tongue.
Pulling the teeth from my gums,
I would decorate the outside of the box,
making patterns of teeth and their many marks.
A latch would be configured with the pieces of broken ribs,
once the most secure of parts because they caged a heart.
I'd lock it with a sealing kiss,
lay it down to sleep in the backyard, with quiet prayers,
under a sky of voyeuristic stars
unable to look away from the unloveliness of this catastrophe.

Exodus

I’ll wait to see your lit cig tip in the dark
to know it’s safe to come home,
the walls not so empty or threatening,
not left to my own thoughts and the tempting
edges of misery I can’t break myself of.
It’s my small heretical version of following fire
and smoke from slavery to promise,
beating evil memories with a stick
to make waters part toward some other future.
Home is protected by prayers
that echo with wails and angry sobs,
plaguing walls with questions tenfold.
The walls held up with dented beams
from pounding questions,
support a roof of smoke built by your lips,
the most stable place I’ve known
curled within your words and breath.
I’ve claimed my release,
following flickers long waited for across
deserts and parted seas, searching for a place
to remove shoes, have a hand to hold mine,
declare the running done and home found.

Heartbroken Whimsy

There is a cut on my wrist over the place
I've considered getting a heart tattooed.
From the cut, blood streams out
in red ribbons intertwined with sinewy threads,
spreading out into a delirious cheshire cat grin.
I pull on the ribbons and feel myself endlessly unravel,
the inside rushing out with a static electric snap on raw skin.
The ribbon spreads out over the floor of my room,
coils and curls into glistening pools
from which purple-leaved trees spring up
with black bark that would blend into any night.
Yellow finches, a thousand years old,
live amidst the purple leaves, clamoring noisily,
their songs echoing in the cavern of the room.
One of the finches flies up to one of my fingers,
transforms into the likeness of a woodpecker
and pecks a hole in my finger's tip.
Out of the hole float luminous colored bubbles,
shiny with possibility, light with something like hope,
floating up to decorate the ceiling
like kites polka dotting the spring sky,
tethered to little kids by pretty green strings.
Blue-eyed spiders also crawl out of the hole in my finger,
making glittery black webs between the purple trees,
swinging from their self-made vines
above the glimmering ribbon pools,
staring at their red tinged reflections.
One bold little spider borrows a yellow feather
from a thousand year old finch,
dips it in the ribbon pool and paints my nails red,
wishing me sweet remembrances of this whimsically awful place

before crawling back inside my finger,
turning the feather into a needle
and sewing the hole closed with its glittery black vines.
I can feel it shimmy down the inside of my finger,
through the internal terrain of my palm and into my wrist,
where the spider again goes to work, sewing me up from inside,
this time using pretty green strings
to close up where a heart still could be.

Mistakes and Darkened Shapes

There are not reasons enough to make it worthwhile,
no apologies for a sinking sun or rising moon,
no sky illuminated sufficiently by stars to change the mind,
only mistakes and darkened shapes,
air filled with smoke and unforgiveness.
Void of grace, enriched with terror,
no way to escape the womb of this trauma,
it makes no fucking sense. Language doesn't exist
in the primordial ooze that drips
onto a linoleum floor from between beaten knees,
the aftermath of nonsensical tremors
and the soulful quaking of cracking bones.
Belonging to the tops of swaying trees at dusk,
the murmur of horrors coming on the windy
precursor to a storm of sunless dark
and long enduring night that ends only with
the conclusion of time that ticks away every merciful glimmer.
Here eyes are built of steel and wire,
hearts of paper mache, all pressed into corners
with hopeless vision and the naked quiver of beating life
which bleeds out in a pool, poisonous to the touch,
the stench of birth and fated death declared
with years pressed into mistaken nights of loathing.
There is never enough trust to hold a promise tight,
keep it safely in growing light, only black assurances remain,
outliving the heaving pangs, the contractions of impending end.

Her Soundtrack

Pressed to the wall, put through a window,
history is made in the mosaic of broken glass.
The soundtrack of time is recorded
in screams echoing up the chimney,
cries breathed into damp pillows.
She is a paper cut wrapped in plastic,
a bloody bolt of lightning against
a thin, pale, print swirled sky.
A dent in the wall, the outline of her body,
chalky portrayals of the day,
and a whisper of exposed secrets.
She reopens the paper cut in order to watch it bleed,
leaving discarded plastic on the bathroom sink.
It rains a little and her blood
becomes a watered down pink
and she remembers princesses from before
she was old enough to handle glass.
Crying wasn't stifled until the age of three
when music became the sound of a panic beaten heart,
the hollows of the walls taking in hushed whimpers
and the repetitive nature of counting.
Now percussion is added with shattered glass,
plaster wall cracking and the flickering
of a chain smoking lighter.
And number eight is on repeat,
the primal scream never before loosed,
now obsessively indulged with veracity
painted red and wrapped in dirty paper cut plastic.

Crash and Burn

I have developed a frightful dependence on the crash and the burn,
that's not to say it doesn't hurt, doesn't cause me to tremble
and quake, but I've become fondly accustomed
to bloody headprints on pounded walls and the stench of burning
so thick it's tasted down the back of my throat.
I don't handle it well when this impact is denied,
like a lot of scotch with no buzz, when this darkness
so rich is absent. I am built upon its presence,
so continual and constant, unending in pressing in, bleeding out,
the forever torturous bouncing between the paradoxical extremes
of smallest vein and artery, wobbling stupor and straight up sobriety.
I am more beautiful wearing a scowl than I'll ever be
with cheeks dimpled by a smile, more reliably stable
in steady pessimism, unshocked by the perpetual knocks and blows.
I am settled by the shaking sky of storms,
the rise of steamy flames from rain pelted hot pavement,
the discomfort of feet scalded by summer blacktop
or the tremble of cold numbed fingers when gloves are too thin
battling ice and the house creaks and groans
with those pains I cannot express for myself.
It's why I keep a razor in an empty Zoloft bottle,
next to the bottles of the blue pills and the yellow, just in case,
occasionally needing something more potent, something
more severe, something requiring no prescription
or interaction with my pharmacist,
just a tissue to catch the tears running down arms and legs.
More often I opt to sit on the back steps, taste the humid air
or be chilled by cooler nights when bare feet hit concrete,
fiddle with a lighter flame that dances with fingers,
get lost in the bright spot of pain on fingerprints,
in the more sinister look of red painted nails

that tempt memories of bloodier nights and days,
but tonight only sizzle and pop with the smell
of their subtle burning. I am so dependent on this crash and burn,
on punching to develop bruises, the sacred marks of impacted life,
on continually fucking it all up because it's all shit anyway and
I'm not sure I believe in getting better, in the possibility
of improving days, believing even less in improving nights,
nights when I toy with ideas of mixing up
the bottles in the cabinet the next morning, the blue, the yellow,
the silver stained red snapped out of a pencil sharpener,
grab one and take whatever is inside, take it deep
with fervency unrivaled, with the liveliness of unwavering decision,
crash and burn, leave skid marks on mapped paradoxes of my arms,
or fall from these heights as the blue or yellow kicks in,
calm the fuck down for a while, tempt ideas of better days,
until the colors become less vibrant
in my blood and, the night, it goes red again.

Swallowing Stars

I wonder what it would be like
to swallow a star each evening,
let the points perforate holes in my spirit
as it tumbles down and through me,
opening up spaces for honest dreams to escape
and fill the room around my bed.
Light and darkness could dance freely
and I would sleep soundly,
freed from unconscious things
so loosed to play themselves out.
Each morning I would sweep up the remnants,
the glitter and the blood, the light and shadow,
medicate my punctures and cover them with bandaids.
It would be a worthy price to pay to swallow purity in the darkness,
banish the tremor of nightmares with a freckle of the night sky.
Some nights a star would go down especially well,
mixed with the red scream of wine lingering on my bedside table,
a perfect match, a way to intensify alcohol's effect,
letting it leak through holes into the core of me
where it can buzz and loosen all constraints,
allow for magic to move through me
and kiss the night with subtle peace.
I would like to pluck a star from the sky,
lift one shot by God's rifle from where it landed,
and take it in as I lay myself to sleep,
let it be a prayer released into the night
as well as the answer received, the kiss on the forehead
and divine wish for sweeter dreams.

He Didn't Hold Her Hand

It's the morning after another
night he didn't hold her hand,
and still she can't stop smiling,
recounting the times he turned
to say hi and look at her with those eyes.
Walking down autumnal paths,
hands in his pockets,
leaves crunching underfoot,
she couldn't help the frequent
glance to watch his profile,
lit by streetlamps and the moon.
Words timed by street crossing
countdowns, it's always
only a matter of time,
just a matter of timing and words
to say what already is.
A text from the next seat over,
wanting to hold her hand,
but he won't, just friends,
or not, or just for now.
Just as friends,
going for a late night walk
down crisp October blocks,
lightened by gin and tonics,
quietly kissing cigs of the same brand.
Just as friends, sideways looks
over crunching leaves,
through timed words,
only a matter of time, for now
walking with hands in pockets
and smiling all the morning after.

TORI LANE

As a Preschool Teacher

There are days when no amount of coffee
can make the day start as it should, with enough energy to face
the onslaught of fourteen four year olds invading the classroom.
There are days when from the first fifteen minutes
sights are already fixed at the point beyond the hand holding
and the glue wiping and the coat zipping, the line leading,
the quiet shushing, song singing, book reading, lunch opening,
lysoling, redirecting, redirecting,
sending to time out of the school day
to that first moment alone in the car
where tears can flow forth freely
or to the dark enfolded evening when a beer, bottle of wine
or the whiskey bottle is brought out,
opened, poured, and consumed.
An exhausting, awkward job just to pay the bills,
a job others think is cute and quaint
and deserving of their voices raising an octave,
like you yourself are one of the four year olds you teach
or the doted upon family pet. But it has its subtle rewards
of little hands seeking yours while walking down the hallway,
the screamed hellos when spotted across the parking lot
or unexpectedly in a public place,
the scribbled pictures of who-knows-what
that they slaved over for excruciatingly long minutes just for you.
And there's the hug of little arms around thighs,
be it received with morning greetings
or before running out the door at day's close,
sought after a fall on the mulch-floored playground
or exchanged in the sporadic collisions
of little student and teacher amidst the happenings of the day.
The best is the little boy who yells goodbye across the room

and leaves with mom, then returns, bounding across the room
once again: *a big hug is coming your way, Miss Tori*
It is the highlight of any day. Along with the proud smile
of writing their name almost right for the first time –
so what if the *d* is flipping backwards into a *b*,
at least its lower case
as the letters following the first are supposed to be.
Or so we're told. And so we tell the preschoolers,
who would curse if they knew how to,
as they struggle with starting at the top of a letter
and going down to kiss the page's many practice lines.
It's a miraculous kind of reward
when they glimmer with getting it –
or almost getting it –
whether they, or we, understand why it needs to be gotten at all.
There are days when it makes no sense
why this is the job that pays the bills,
why it has to be the not so cute and certainly not quaint job
of searching for marker tops, wiping down tables,
opening apple sauce, trying to dodge the spray of little sneezes,
helping with belt buckles and shoelaces –
a job where the expression about herding cats
makes more sense than walking one foot in front of the other.
There are days when the kids need no time outs,
but teacher does, a moment in the hallway to breathe,
to lock away the frustrated tears, to reapply the smile –
the one energized and genuine from the first day of school,
the one slowly suffocating with all the disinfecting spray
and squished under a tumbling tower of wooden blocks.
There are days when vision is impaired more by tears
than rain on the windshield or the slowly sagging sun
and the inevitable questions of how to make it to summer
swirl around with the wine in the nearly empty

glass at the end of the day. But there are moments in those days,
moments when a little girl begs you to read a story
and she will not be satisfied until you are not just reading,
but she's sitting in your lap while you do so,
when one of them screams your name across the room
and you can't be angry
because he just wants to show you
the barely legible name he's written on his paper,
when a little boy runs back into the classroom to give you a hug,
when one of them turns around during lunch
and quietly says *I love you* just because,
when you pull out a small stack of scribbled pictures at home,
with different moderately readable names
spattered across their corners,
some slightly misspelled, and you can't help but smile
as you pull a beer from the fridge
and begin to hang them all on its outside.

Follow

Follow the smoke of your voice into the hallways
of the night and you will be persuaded
of your eternal worth and the uncontrollable
value of questioning all things.
Yesterday didn't exist well, today
failed to perform its functions of memory,
tomorrow will dawn with new destructions
and an inscrutable lack of answers.
I have become more than I was meant to be,
caged in the holes of your chest,
dancing in the smoke you suck in.
I will breathe it out. You follow the stars
on a motionless journey toward
nothing you know of but all you hope for in redemption.
I self-destruct inside you and you leave me behind,
bread crumbs marking the yesterdays
you leave. I am the trail you've walked
and I've tasted the smoke of your lungs.
Walk through our shared taste and you'll know
what I never knew, never learned. It is all false,
but more real than you can fathom.
It is fathomless reality beyond your inquiry,
only blindly followed in the night of your leaving.

The Act of Writing

It's hard to write poetry when the roof is being replaced,
a dumpster sitting outside the window, pieces of the roof
being thrown into it,
fluttering and crashing with the unexpectedness
of a body throwing itself from a skyscraper.
There is little inspiring about the large red monstrosity,
chipped and dirty, being filled with the flimsy pieces
of what once protected, sheltered, covered.
Awareness of vulnerability grows, rumbling
in the sounds of workmen, echoing in the caverns of heart,
reflecting off the page or the cursor blinking screen,
calling for a confession.
The writer is called to give voice
to that which the writer alone loves,
to give voice to one's own astonishment, or so says Annie Dillard.
It's like standing naked on the lawn,
sharing your physical self with the world,
letting all the embarrassing bulges receive sun and
the shadows of curves refuse it.
It's like the dressing room door flying open mid-change
or being walked in on in a public restroom.
It's getting caught in a downpour wearing a white shirt or
discovering your fly is down and
it's probably been that way for hours.
It's the redlikethedumpster faced humiliation
of unexpected vulnerability,
not always pretty, but always honest.
No wonder the writing process is painful.
It's scaling the outside of a skyscraper. Naked.
The magnificent skill or unrefined desperation required to climb
coupled with total exposure makes for an exhausting venture.

FALLING SEASON

It’s rewarding when the skyline is seen, unadulterated wind and sun
caress bare skin, and the task is done. Astonishment voiced.
But sometimes, too aware of the vulnerability
of having the roof removed above you,
you’d more readily throw yourself from the top.

TORI LANE

Andrea's Blue Blanket

I woke up feeling a little like hell,
because now unremembered dreams disturbed my full night sleep,
hard sleep, through the night sleep, instead waking up
every time my body demanded a repositioning sleep.
My morning mug filled with darkness couldn't
chase away the monsters,
the monsters unseen, leaving me feeling unclean
so I showered,
stripped naked in the bright light of afternoon sun
streaming through the window in the bathroom
like the light through the window of my childhood bedroom
with its once hideous wallpaper before being painted white,
the afternoon light that illuminated bright
things of which I do not wish to speak.
I showered, did my hair, put on make up, clothes and boots –
the old men's boots I wore in androgynous high school days
with scuffed toes that look like they should be steel toed
but they aren't, but I pretended they were,
like I pretended I was tough enough to deal with the world
when I was silently falling apart
under the weight of the things of which I do not wish to speak.
I laced up the boots just to get back on my bed,
have an identity crisis as memory returned,
clashed with that moment, crashed and burned.
Watching poets on youtube throughout the afternoon,
I watched Andrea Gibson perform *Blue Blanket*,
had no idea that she'd poetically and boldly speak
of the things I do not want to.
Only afterwards when I googled the words
did I find the warning of triggers for those left behind
in the wake of the things of which I still do not wish to speak

but she did and she didn't just speak
she almost sang, creating a melody for my pain
that I'd rather ignore, pretend I am past
but obviously I'm not
'cause I grabbed coat and keys,
bolted out the door, drove to this coffee shop
with the best brew in town
and I sit staring down into this notebook
scrawling away about the unprepared for shock of the day
and the words she damn near sang,
the words that reminded me I was almost broken –
almost, not quite,
'cause I'm still learning to fight to get out of bed in the morning
or in the late afternoon,
to dance, quietly swaying in the backyard
under the not yet full moon,
to find safety in this body,
this body I hate but am learning to embrace,
quietly, gently, softly,
like fingers scooping up a crippled-winged moth
from the sidewalk, with kinder fingers and touches
than this often hated, sometimes embraced body can recall.
I realize I don't have any idea at all how to make it,
but bury it and keep trying to fake it,
until days like today when someone rips open my insides
with a jagged blue blanket
and reminds me I was almost broken,
almost broken, but not quite.

TORI LANE

The Voice

It's loud enough to tremble in my coffee
but still soft enough to quell the mistrust of the beating rhythm
of this rapidly aging and cracking heart.
Echoing within my breath, woven between my fingers,
I could be unsure of where I begin and end,
my lips wrapped around the sound,
made one and nearly the same.
It's the gap in the swirling clouds,
the clarity within the ceaseless raging
that whispers between flashes and rumbles.
The voice dances, intertwined with my steps,
causing me to stumble into a new tempo,
unfamiliar, unsteady, beautiful.
I am unsure of where I begin and end,
where my feet actually meet the ground,
conceding to movement and brief still moments.

Hard Kiss Goodnight

There is a hole in my head and it cries
like its dead, descending into hell, no more hope,
no turning back. It's a mouth full of truth, raging
real with its screams, getting loud about its darkness,
it's hell while still alive – wanting out, to make it stop,
to make out with a gun and swallow hard the pill
of its one loud lie. The metallic bang would go down
sweeter than all tasteless days so dulled
by the discordant gore of pornographic memory.
Any lie would taste better than the decades old
truth of knowing the taste of a child, of being a child
many times tasted, of all the lip contorted silences and
these days now of wanting cleaner air that never comes.
Each breath is like smoke, choked on but taken down,
like the burn of whiskey from its bottle's throat.
That burn is no longer enough, wanting the one
fast peck, powder flash, the short hard kiss goodnight
that blows the mind out the back of the head, promising
this too hard reality can be dead, a new painted gore
on the wall of some room, on the grassy floor of some day,
knowing this one stupid way to escape from this living hell
is to French a silver hand held bitch and swallow
just one little lie.

Spell It Out

Use your words, baby girl, spell it out, make it known,
those things you refuse to say as if no words existed
to contain what was held behind doors.
Use your words, throw open the door,
rip it off the hinges and dismantle the locks
on the language you've grown in passing time.
Mature to a state where you can devolve into memory,
go behind the door that wasn't opened fast enough
and press in unknown words to make it real,
make it wrong, make it not your fault.
Use your words, baby girl, no, it's not your fault,
no, you aren't that girl, never meant to be.
Spell it out, let me know what happened there,
throw your tantrum now and let it fly
out windows, out of doors,
let it hit the fucking sky with a bolt of light
and the deep throated scream that's been waiting to escape
from behind the unopened door with its first gust of fresher air
and first gasp of words to call it all that it fucking was.
I invite you to cry, go ahead.
I beg you to let loose, let it echo in the hallways,
down the stairs, through every room of the house,
that most necessary wail you've stifled.
There is no need to stifle it now, let it out,
baby girl, let it out, you don't have to be so strong,
you are allowed to fall apart,
bang on the walls and floors, break things,
just not yourself, you've been broken enough,
but you aren't damaged goods, don't ever believe
you are damaged goods, baby girl.
You are enough, worth the weight of truthful words

to be a battering ram at the door,
crushing the secrecy you don't need to hold onto anymore.
Let it out, speak up, use the words you've learned with years,
go back and beat the hell out of what's unseen,
splatter abusive blood on walls with the words.
Spell it out, let it be real,
let yourself hurt, baby girl, let yourself heal.

TORI LANE

Wallpaper

It was blue and mildly hideous,
though I didn't recognize that then.
The lower portion was two toned –
a darker blue for outlined boats,
a lighter blue of backsplash –
the upper portion, subtly patterned with delicate dots.
The bordered middle held the mediocre life of the wall
with its scene:
        a large ship leaving port,
        a woman in 1920s garb
        waving a handkerchief,
        goodbye to someone
        tucked mysteriously out of sight.
I would stretch my little body out
on my bed for hours, staring at the wallpaper:
tracing lines between dots and boats,
dreaming up the unseen other,
creating stories of beautifully tragic goodbyes.
        I could've been lost for days in the wallpaper blues.

Over the years the blues came to hold
a great depth of secrets.
Uncried tears were pressed into dots.
My romanticized notions were hidden
away on the boats sailing the lower halves of my walls.
Something important was sealed up
in the large ship
        and I was the woman waving a tragic goodbye.

To say innocence was the important something
sealed up in the ship and sent out to sea or

that important something lost seems cliché –
like innocence was left on a restaurant table,
found missing when I returned to retrieve it,
or it was attached to the car keys that never
made it to the counter where they belonged,
or innocence simply fell through a hole in my pocket,
unbeknownst to me,
and there is no way of knowing where it slipped out.
But innocence didn't disappear from where it should've been
or fall out of a pocket
or tragically and romantically sail out to sea on a ship.
It was slapped around,
beaten into a corner by a belt with a fat buckle
and made to cry,
mutilated into a pitiable state
beyond recognition by even me
who had possessed it since birth.
It bled into those wallpaper blues
        and there surrendered its own fucking existence.

Epiphany

Fossilized memory was shared and something
shook in the tombs of my chest,
changing a twistedly compassionate heart to quivering stone.
The tremendous energy swirled and trembled in my core,
convulsed through limbs, filled lungs with pressure
and embedded a desire for noise in my long silent tongue.
It murmured new intensities until I was so nauseated by my history,
I threw memory into the sky and the blue shattered,
like a rock through a flock of birds,
a brick through a window, a bullet through a head.
The blue fell in mirrored shards until only
the star freckled black remained.
It screamed with the dazzling clarity of naked rage,
of uncovered glories, of mystically known truth.
Only the rim of this raw expression has been known til now,
too entangled in constraining light to see the honesty of raging life,
to dip into the darkness glittered with the vibrant specks
of unconcealed primal screaming.
This is more authentic living, walking on
a mosaic of blue mirrored sky,
under a brilliant clarity of darkness
from which entombed stars do not shy from screaming.

Dealing

Burn down your childhood home,
set ablaze the formative memories
in all their terrible glory.
Learn to look them in the eye and say,
Fuck it.
Throw the panic to the wind
as the match hits the pavement
and your history meets flames.
You've become good at such introductions,
forcing reality to drown in fire,
giving words to the horrors,
and you stand by silently with near vacant eyes,
hardly hearing the screams as the violence of truth
meets the violence of memory
and the latter is raped into submission.
There is no name strong enough to take in the heat,
no image brazen enough to burn away
what was forcefully imprinted.
Light a cigarette with the edge of your destruction,
taste revenging misery roll up against
the mistrust of your years,
forging new safety with the outpouring of smoke.

Star Points

I lay down on the carpet and stare up through the window,
watch light and color drain from the world
and stars begin to poke holes in the dark.
The stars tremor and move for me,
pitying my lonely state,
offering their condolences for my tragedies.
The stars break off their many pointed corners
and bleed streaks into the night,
tell me I'm not alone in the hurt,
tell me to brand red circles onto my skin
and remember what now remains of them.
To remember all their empathetic streaks in the dark,
their shakes and tremors,
the way they enter into my dirt bound world
and let their lights get muddied
just so they can sit with me a while.
They press their broken points into my hands,
cutting gently into my skin,
their starlit blood mingling a bit with mine
in hopes that I might glow a little,
I might hope a little,
I might see light in myself
and poke holes in my own darkness.
They hang themselves from my ceiling,
dangle above my bed,
so I can turn off the lights, pull shut the blinds,
and lay under a red streaked, empathetic night
in the early pieces of morning and in mid afternoon,
rubbing my fingers over the scabs in my palms,
remembering how they tried to push light into me.
I put the broken points in my pockets,

feel them stab my legs with each daily step,
pull them out sporadically to pinch them between fingers,
spread them out on a table and slide them around,
dotting the table with red fingerprints,
remembering how the stars came to sit with me a while,
how they broke themselves and now hang from my ceiling.
The points press into my fingertips,
embed themselves under my swirling prints,
and I tap them on the table, feeling stabs of their light,
try to mimic them and poke holes in the darkness.

Makeshift Home

I still dream in incisions and stitches,
of the former blades and metal of my trade
when unhindered I'd work grooves into my skin,
toy always with light and dark,
and find the depths of which I'm made,
unsure if I'd survive my young life,
if I'd ever be more than the sum of the scarring marks.
With tattoo ink I protect myself from my ungodly urges,
keeping skin clean from the blood
that surges from self inflicted grooves and gashes
that once so littered my skin,
letting out what was once locked up,
so tightly held in under silent years
when I tried to forget the realities
of every parent's fears,
my innocence evicted, sent packing,
and I was learning the art of stacking
brick upon brick, stone upon stone,
to build up walls and try to forget.
I painted the walls of my makeshift home
with the colors of a lie,
pretending everything was alright,
yes, everything is fine,
I am alive, but I filled the cracks with my blood,
and each dream flooded with images
of nooses and knives, of death,
the cessation of the breath I never enjoyed,
never took deeply, only took in weakly
as the first weeks stretched into years
and I learned how to stifle my tears.
Keep them behind the walls, unheard, unseen,

and everyone will believe you are still clean,
purity intact, because it's only that fact that matters.
It's been a long time since I've been that clean,
before the smoking and drinking,
the depressed nights of sinking into my skin
whatever I could find that would let out that sin,
what so long was held in,
inside the walls of my makeshift home,
built brick by brick and stone by stone.
It's the safest reality I have known,
found in the depths under skin,
in the grooves letting me see within,
letting out the pulse of life of which I'm made
with the various tools of my ungodly trade,
one I learned on my own, my own sacred craft
within these cold walls of stone,
more of a tomb than a home,
I've been here slowly dying under the colors
of my lying and pretending,
from the metal descending into the depths,
exploring how I am made.
I no longer engage those things,
but I'm still far from entirely saved,
not yet safe in my own skin
because I still long for those incisions,
those grooves and gashes made so masterfully,
birthed in painful mystery, in the darkness of my secrecy.
I awake each day to new destruction,
in memory and haunted thoughts
of digging down to find the depths of imperfection,
searching out what is cradled in the deep,
letting out what I have learned to keep silent.

Still in Bed

The weight of this almost summer heat is oppressive
and it suits me well, far better than the cool perfection
of last week's high 70s, light breeze, cloud accented sky.
The green of the trees and colors of blooms have been sickening,
too damn sweet, but in the humid discomfort of this evening,
it's now possible to venture outside beyond the tug
of mere obligation because it feels like I'm still wrapped up,
cozy, disconcertingly warm in my bed, my afternoon and
evening residence of weeks and too many eye drooling hours.
It seems I've lost control –
my eyes becoming ever running faucets, not dripping, but
overflowing the bathtub and flooding the whole damn house.
My mind has been playing with nooses, driving off cliffs and
weighted in the bottom of that tub, blowing less than desperate
bubbles, a slow gurgling release without the vaguest hint
of putting up a fight. This mind of mine wanders
down darkened corridors caked with the blood
of not quite suicidal intentions, not wanting to die,
just to turn off for a bit, forget about existing
for a handful of days, wrapped up in the sheets
of a solitary room, pretending each breath doesn't hurt,
the sun doesn't blind and each smiling face isn't a slap to mine.
Today I haven't bothered with covering up the dark circles
under eyes or trying to perk up the weighted drag to my walk,
instead I've moved from the full sized bed in the corner
of my room into the fuller spaces of thick, almost summer air.
It's easier to be out when all distinctions are fading,
when my bed is the world I've been residing in and
the world begins to mimic the cave of my wrinkled
sheet covered bed. All things have begun to blur, receding
into each other, day and night, moments and hours, despair

and hope, inside and out. Outside but entirely curled up in
my interior that is losing distinctions
but still it has plenty of walls to bang my head against
with a thud, thud, thud that echoes inside
the cavernous space of me. But it may not be the sound
of my head's impact with walls, rather the sound of my heart
forcing blood to move, to keep me alive, to keep moving –
come on, keeping moving! I give myself a headache
with these walls, listening to the beating that goes with me
from one internal space to the more expansive next,
from one private residence to a larger one that feels dreadfully,
blissful the same. Nothing changes,
or nothing seems to, even as I relocate,
my mind still wanders and eyes still leak,
and the bathtub keeps filling and the floors are getting all wet.

Slowly, Slowly

Wipe the cold rain from my eyes,
blow the smoke and dust from lungs,
it could be time to pull the anchor up from the dry ground,
move slowly forward with the tick tocking time
of a swinging hammock, of slow rolling tears.
Through the youngest of eyes discern character,
unearth all the unfathomable reasons for loving well,
see through heaven's veil with four-year-old simplicity
and discover the fabric of which I'm quilted together,
what loving unseen hands could've held close,
kissed goodnight, good morning, My love,
wrapped with black night flecked with stars
before pressing me down under the globe of day,
placed in the autumn leaves and crisp air.
Slowly, slowly, with dying leaves, my colors can change,
revealed with the uncertainty of beautiful questions
and breaking loose the rusty anchor chain,
screaming from the balcony toward the geese
I want to chase into the air and watch fly away.

Means of My Love

Frayed around these edges, unbearably thin have I become,
so fragile with the unraveling,
disseminating thoughts and pieces that dangle
from these wiry threads, purple and blue
like the sacred bruise worn on knuckles slammed
repeatedly into hardwood realities.
The bruise is the mark of connection,
wiry arms reaching from spirit to the world of concrete artifact,
making me a person of actual size, of weighty sensuality,
known not in loveliness but violence. This is how I exist
and these are the means of my love,
but only insofar as love can be defined as dutiful attention
with no definite descriptors of the character of that attention,
letting attention be the fact of my knowing
rather than the sanctity of its intention.
Love will be defined by its force in color,
its pressure into the unbearable thinness of these days,
days where skin clings close to bone, lips curl
tightly around sound and essential things fall
from fingers unfurled from well loved knuckles
at the extended ends of wiry arms, arms fragile
but defined with tension,
like the edges of weary days unbearable,
that is, if days can so be called weary,
as if they can be worn down by their inevitable progressions,
as if they could tire at all. It's the same question to pose of skin,
if it would wear out from the force of connection,
from such dutiful attentions, from the repeated impact of love,
if this loving could ever too much,
to be worn thin and deep with color.

The Last Pack of Cigarettes

I pull myself from the pack each time I remove
a cigarette to set quietly aflame.

Somehow, I am the small length of addictive indulgence
held carelessly between my fingers,
with no actual regard, near indifference,
yet I consistently fail to part with myself,
an addict of my own continued existence.

I am the smoke that floats away from my lips and disperses.

I try to put memories in my mouth,
encourage the smoke to carry it out onto the air, away from me,
but it's only smoke that leaves on the wind.

I am the flick of ash, the slight tremble of fingers –
I twitch and shake, fall to kiss the ground
and see that my skin still bleeds.

I am also the long slow drag, the burn out of nostrils,
the intimate touch of chapsticked lips to the filter.

Now barely alight, I am the ugly nub near that filter,
that which needs to be thrown down to meet ashes, disregarded.

I am mostly this – the disregarded.

I am the allure, the disgust,
the draw in and loathing push away.
I am first glance beautiful, ugly at least, fatal at best,
unneeded, barely wanted, but purchased still.

FALLING SEASON

Tonight, under a swooning navy sky with a round glowing moon,
I pull out the last cigarette in the pack,
set myself alight and take in a last first breath of myself.
I sit on the front steps, offer no word,
only memories to be let loose on smoke.

It's comforting to reach the ugly nub of disregard,
to throw myself on the sidewalk at my feet
and press the last bit of flame out of me.

Identities

I am unsettled contradictions. I am all settled contradictions. I am far more than I think I am. I am never enough. I am real, but nonexistent. I am little more than fiction and the boldest of brazen fact. I am older than I look, younger than I feel. I am invisible. I am nakedly seen. I am all skin and bone. I am the most lusciously full of flesh. I am curves and straight lines, angles, ridges and swirls. I am the wanted unknown and the known unwanted. I am molested, untouched, too fully known, a mystery. I am violated, carrying taintedness into the safety of new spaces. I am now safe, but still not yet. I am a repressor of memories who still remembers too much. I am a deep hole of memory to be fallen into, I never know when to expect the bottom to break my fall, as well as my bones. I am broken pieces of my former whole. I am made of young creaking bones, cracked with an agedness of spirit. I am the remaining – the remaining, unwhole, a divided aged soul. I exist more deeply than I should. I am me but not entirely myself. I am someone else. I am madness with a lucid mind. I am an explorer of worlds. I am the cowardice of ages. I am happily lost. I am uncontentedly found. I am repentant, forgiven and yet unredeemed. I am ceaseless motion, the dance of future dreams. I am personified stillness, with the deep roots of an oak tree. I am an illogical dreamer, searching depths and heights, but I never wander far from home. I am barefoot in the rain, t-shirt in the snow, hand close to the fire. I am completely sober, entirely intoxicated. I am built of despair, a conduit of hope. I am a voiceless speaker, an unspoken voice. I speak a thousand soulful languages but I never make a sound. I am silence enfleshed and I carry a loud yell in my chest. I am full to explosion. I am a deep breath never taken, deflated lungs grieving ageless emptiness. I am made up of screaming, silent canyons – the places that once held innocence, promise, hope. I am a raging entombed in skin. I am all horror, a quiet taste of loveliness. I am more than pretty, less than beautiful, a most hideous thing to be seen. I am an old soul cultivated by sadness and secrets. I am all things tremendous. I am nothing at all.

I Mourn

I mourn the day of meeting,
when I befriended the future orchestrator of my nightmares.
I mourn that worst day of my young life
though I loved it then.
I mourn the memories made solely in body
as the rest of me learned to disconnect and hide,
the simplicity too early lost and sick complexity gained.
Our split connection, I mourn it too,
and the half I too willingly took for myself,
all the blame and shame that were never mine to take.
I mourn the day I finally learned its name.
I mourn the subsequent years of silence and of sinking,
hiding, pretending, wishing away a reality
I couldn't wholly ignore.
I mourn years of bleeding sin not mine
out of my skin and hoping I'd somehow feel clean.
I mourn my keeper's life,
how I've kept the secrets in a locket
hanging above my caged heart and below my conscious mind,
with all the vividness of my dreams and nightmares of my days.
I mourn my reintegrating self, the pain of being whole
when I can't remember ever being whole before,
the way the memories of body are now leaking into spirit
and being lived all over again.
I mourn the entirety of life, so totally unlived,
my quarter century of existing more dead than alive.
I mourn it in tears, in silence,
in the shaking stillness of body.
I mourn it in red, in black, in bruising blue,
in splattered tones, in the electric scream of yellow.
I have come to mourn the very air I breathe,

what fills and propels me now, and even more so
that first breath after birth with which I declared my living.
I mourn each of my moments from that first breath
until that day of meeting.
I mourn the child that was, the blue eyed innocence.
I mourn the child that died.
I mourn because no one else ever noticed she'd gone.

TORI LANE

Outlet

There is an outlet on the ceiling, ten feet high in
the window of this place, between two yellow lights
hanging over the little tables next to me.
It's a bizarre place for an outlet and I can't help but wonder
why it is there, what purpose could such an oddly placed
fixture serve – for the *open* sig this place doesn't have,
for the twinkling holiday lights taped up all winter,
or maybe for an orange extension cord
with which to make a noose and hang all these inquiries of mine,
try to put them eternally to neck broken rest.
After all, what makes me tip back my head and stare
at the ceiling rather than focusing on the drink in my hand
or reading the book on my table, or listening in
on the conversation of the two elderly women behind me,
or staring at the people walking by outside, beyond the glass,
crossing the lines between shadows and sun?
Maybe I'd rather see the unseen, rebel against the simple
in the pursuit of something more deeply complex.
I no longer look at my feet when I walk, am no longer content
with eye level observations, rather looking up,
around, inside, asking questions that maybe don't have answers,
that maybe shouldn't be asked, but I ask them all the same,
head tilted back to look at what holds the places above me,
eyes closed to see what is hidden with different eyes,
those of reckless, insatiable curiosity.
Maybe I want to be contrary for the sake of it,
do what I've been told not to,
figure things out for myself, beat my way
to my own belief through the medicated haze
of what's been prescribed for me. I think I believe
more fully in finger painting, puddle jumping and

earning good bruises than in looking good
and being an adult as I'm told. The bruise and scrape
are somehow sacred, colored vibrant marks of life,
proof of risks taken, mistakes both deep and shallow
but undoubtedly made, seen on my skin.
Jesus said that thing about abundant life and
I've extrapolated its meaning
in those colors of clumsiness and violence that scream
of movement and play, of a fiercely honest exploration of life.
Some Sunday mornings are better spent in the rain by the river
than in the pews of a sanctuary. I meet God in the mud,
where I am as I am, sometimes there more earnestly myself,
with uncovered bruises and scrapes,
with mud on my feet and rain in my hair, eyes sweating tears
and lips oozing laughter. I prefer making church there
or in talking to wonderful strangers or playing on a playground
or around a table, where there is wine with dinner and communion
in the hearts behind the words of conversation. Those words
create worlds in which to build cities, places to reside,
and I'd rather live there,
connected and bruised, muddied and marked well.

Eggshells

The jagged pieces quiver and skitter across the night,
the wall fallen eggshells trampled by a royal stampede.
Things are better left scattered for a while,
don't put me back together again,
let me soak in this weary reality,
remembering with words formerly unspoken,
now felt beyond the grasp of time.
I will be an eggshell mosaic, broken pieces
mixed with glittered stars and well worn pearls.
It's the becoming of more than these fears,
tracking down distant hopes,
creating something new of these fragile pieces
broken at the base of bricks and mortar,
blown over by wind and rain,
but reconciled with a new living form of beauty.

Ella

The skin of her face cracks open in a smile
that lifts the day, pulls it back in a slingshot
and sends it careening forward
with precious energy and laughter.
Walking slowly to the playground,
far behind the rest of the class,
she pauses to kick the leaves off the sidewalk,
mimicking what I'd done the day before,
each time she giggles and a piece falls into place
in the puzzling question of why I've remained.
For these months I am hers, gratefully possessed
in focus on what will make her laugh,
on what will make today one of the days
where she sporadically starts dancing with me
to the music only she can hear
but is teaching me to feel in the recesses
of who I am, who I may be called to be.

Art is Order

Dividing the paved street from the dust and dirt of unfinished road,
there are concrete dividers sitting under the stop light,
perpetually flashing red, which is under
the new bridge I like to fly over.
On the concrete dividers, people I'll never meet
have doodled with spray cans,
graffiti I cannot decipher save for the one bold statement in black,
articulated clearly, precisely, atop the rest.
Art is Order the black paint unequivocally declares,
the statement mimicked in strength of letter and line.
Art is order to the one who denied the ordering law
and shook the can, maybe danced to created beat,
painted on the concrete under flashing red lights
that separate the paved roads of completion
from the dust and dirt of the yet to be constructed.
Art is order in the way a heart thumps steadily,
until the day it bows out of the ballroom dance,
the day when it refuses to so much as even sway,
moved by rhythmic melody while standing against the wall.
Art is order in the way snow falls,
wavering between flickering flurries and
large white chunks of molting angels wings falling to earth.
Art is order in the way I've known someone for years
and yesterday was the first time I nearly
choked on the blue of his eyes.
Art is order in the way red wine sits majestically in a glass
and the way it looks like blood,
so blood too must look beautiful in a glass,
swirling out of a bottle into the deathlike stillness of my glass
before being swallowed down to dance with hot, living blood,
the red wine beauty of my veins.

FALLING SEASON

Art is order in the way people pray to an unseen God
but know, they know, they know that unseen divine thing
is more real than any wind turned air
they suck into despairing lungs.
Art is order in the way I,
preschool teacher, seminary student, dancer, poet,
want to be dressed all in black under the star sprayed sky,
dancing to the created beats of a shaking spray paint can,
making bold statements on concrete,
which is firmer than the paper of notebooks
and all the air I've thrown words upon,
dancing in the red glow of flashing lights
under the new bridge I like to fly over.

TORI LANE

But Your Eyes

You catch moments in your teeth and chew them through,
I swallow minutes and hours,
washed down with black coffee,
building a calendar of years in my stomach,
choking on the evenings and mornings with you,
the times in the car and at the bar
with a beer and shot of whiskey.
It burns through me, dizzying vision,
pressing my feet into the ground
and my head into the overcast heavens.
You take the time and devour it,
destroying its constructs and limits,
gnawing through the boundaries and obligations.
Nothing matters but your eyes, the sideways glance
with the power of three Jack and Cokes
chasing a long, empty stomach day.
The days go on too long, but the porch sitting,
Marlboro smoking evenings with you flee rapidly
as the vibrant colors of concluding day.
These days have become freckles in the night,
numerous and hard to focus on,
and I'd rather watch them fly across the sky
in their supposed falling to match mine,
descending into the smallest possible piece of time.
Even those moments of catching fallenness
in the perfected flash of a gaze upward
cannot compare to the extended time of your eyes
when you turn back to wave again in the dark
or to whisper greeting a second time, walking side by side.
Your eyes are clocks with no hands,
counting eternity in heart pulses and beats,

dilated with the unending infinity of a stare
containing stars drowned in whiskey and affections.

Spring Lit Windows

The windows, spring lit, say it’s time to work the line of heart,
yawn and stretch, awake the explorer spirit,
adventure into the simple monotonous beauty of black coffee,
chase granola through yogurt and spill ink on a page.
It is only in these quiet hours,
before the screaming of children into the classroom,
hours of planning and meetings, studying for night classes,
in the stillness of a house still sleeping,
not yet creaking with movement,
that the poet lives and breathes well.
She is made a thief when the world awakes,
stealing the moments of the in betweens,
composing in the purse held notebook
and in the notepad of her phone.
But when the sun tiptoes through windows with spring light
and pulls on the frayed strands of heart,
she rises from sleeping beauty silence
and spreads herself onto the receptive pages
that wait in the earliest hours of morning.

Yellow and Black

Golden finches of the most brilliant hue
have been flocking to my neighbor's birdfeeder.
I sit with the tousled hair and coffee cup of earliest morning
and watch, unable to convince myself to move
or lower my eyes into my book. The flirtatious flashes
of yellow and black dart just beyond the glass,
drawing me to something more slowly hopeful
than the restlessness of dreams and rapid days.
In a storm littered night, black with warnings of rain
and severe wind, I see the same flash as a stoplight turns yellow
and screams against the sky's fiercely possessed dark.
It demands a slowing car on slick pavement
and calls me back to the murmurs of morning light,
to moments slowed into, taken in so deeply
I cannot help but honestly live them through.
The flash sends me rooted into the ground of present time,
immersed in the terror of dark warnings and nights
and in the possibilities of a more truly experienced life.

Autumn's Other Name

I have always loved autumn,
as a word and season,
with its richness of maturing colors,
crisp air and the back to school
freshness that seems to reset everything.
As a word, autumn sounds more graceful,
less ominous than the season's nickname –
the depressing four letter word that calls to attention
the crumbling deterioration of the time.
But this year, I prefer to claim that other name,
explore a season of falling –

falling because I tried.
I accepted challenge.
Even invited it.
I succeeded as well as fucked up.
I played. I tripped and skinned my knees,
wore bandaids over battle scrapes.
I used my imagination –
told stories of fighting dragons, being the princess
and saving my own damn self –
and then returned to less glorious reality.
I opened up to experience,
to loving and its flipside of losing
or the unexpectedness of keeping.
Because I pushed, pursued and
received my own pursuit.
Falling because I stole Icarus' waxen wings,
made his mistake for myself,
just to say I did it, I risked,
I took myself on an adventure,

FALLING SEASON

I lived in honest exploration –
honest like the unassuming surrender
of yellowing leaves from a tree in early September,
pointing to the glorious approach of my falling season.

Tag

I was a little girl who played tag,
who loved playing tag:
freeze tag, TV tag, dance tag, hide and seek tag,
straight up every day run around in circles tag.
Chase, be chased, screaming in the race to home base –
nothing beat the bobbingweavingspinning out of reach
of the one deemed *it*,
feeling the rushing air of reaching hand but no contact with skin
or grabbing of shirt, the joy of the momentary win.
The neighborhood kids would congregate in a chattering clump,
then spread,
a giggling, screaming virus infecting the once quiet corners
behind houses, between parked parental cars,
running across lawns in fanciful maneuvers
that assuredly looked ridiculous.
The flight of running feet made anything permissible,
all things possible,
a superhero in the moments uncaught.
On the quiet afternoons when the others couldn't join,
the blonde best friend and I played around
the patterned line of bushes,
big and green alternating with small and thorny,
that stretched out between her house and the main street.
Up and down the grassy slope, dashing between the bushes,
no home base, quicker turn around, faster pace, quicker collapse
in the exhausted chant of – I quit! I quit! Game over!
I hovered, hiding between alternating bushes one bright
but cloudy day when the blonde best friend flew
shrieking around one, big and green.
I screamed first in the joyous frustration of my foundness and
second in the sharp stab of thorns through clothes

and the rip of exposed skin.
I had maneuvered myself with a spin into
the small thorny bush of the patterned line.
My superhero flight ended with tears
and the pluckingpullingbodysearching process of mom's tweezers.
That thorny mistake, a twisting with fate,
was prophetic though unrealized then –
I would run from the realities of abuse into
the streaks of bloody scratched arms,
though not from mistake or thorn,
but purposeful fingernails, blades and pins,
digging in to deal with the memories I'd made.
I have been a woman playing tag, running from the *it* of memories,
not with laughter and flight, but desperation,
and fear bleeding skin from fingernail, blade
and ironically named safety pin.
I want to stop playing tag, twisting in the thorns,
stop running and face it,
and from that stationary place, staring *it* in the face,
reclaim my superhero status and all the possibilities of flight.

Transformative Motion

Motion equates with change:
pursuing the collisions of impulsiveness and movement
in the improvisation of attentive living –
the brilliant authenticity of rapid design
in the directional movement of change, of journey,
of progressions from that initial beginning point –
a singular point of commonality, all having beginnings,
of various sorts, but beginnings still,
and motion stemming, growing, emerging
from that commonality of pointed place.
Motion equates with change:
moving in unrehearsed honesty, with spontaneity
and responsive awareness,
allowing for expanse and obligatory regressions
in the winding progression of forward life motion.

Khulumani

Names are worn off the soles of our shoes,
wrists wrapped in pearls and scarred hearts,
we hold each other's stories in tears,
and learn to speak our own with uncovered voices.
These stories are shared, all but the same,
but intertwined entirely, completely.
Somehow we are one,
an unlikely family we would never choose
but now could never live without.
We go out together, leaving behind old tremors and doubts
and the echoing chorus of screams from the balcony.
Pushed out of this known seclusion,
we carry new power on tongues, courage in hearts,
well earned exhaustion of spirits,
and *love you* engraved on straighter standing spines.

for the participants, coaches and crew of
H-E-A-R-T's first Victim-to-Victim Retreat (Oct. 2011)

TORI LANE

Hummingbirds

Drink in the sound of cars on the street,
the thumping of the basketball game in the driveway,
the squeal of a swing cradled child,
and so know the loud pressure of a silent moment,
destroy the best painting to learn echoes of mourning,
walk barefoot on hot pavement to understand fragility of body,
paint nails red so when they are flecked
with dirt they look like lady bugs.
This is the way I'll advise my grandchildren
when I'm old and unregretfully grey. I'll tell them
to spend nights under their beds with the monsters,
reading them stories with flashlights and drinking hot chocolate.
Roll in the grassy lawn and try to see how the world rotates,
stand and wobble on their axis, kiss the edges of unseen galaxies.
Have hands that flutter over guitar strings,
turquoise painted hummingbird wings in flight,
emboldened to start a meaningless fight or
to peel the layers of honeysuckle to find its taste,
savoring the hint of things simple but greater than many others.
You see, I believe in carrying a poem
on my tongue rather than in my pocket,
knowing it so I can taste its flavor mingle with each breath,
not just the few I intentionally read it into. It's a way of faith,
not a leap or even a hop, but a stumbling in its general direction.
When they are old enough, taking themselves too damn seriously,
I'll tell them to get one frivolous tattoo they'll slightly regret
and to get at least one they'll love, get a little tipsy some afternoon
and taste the world's elliptical rotation around the sun.
Paint a day by numbers and walk the tight rope of the lines,
dip toes on either side and blur it all together,
muddy the watercolors with preschool frivolity,

declare journaled squiggles to be fine literature,
wear brightly colored bandaids,
drive a little too fast and learn to walk slowly,
listen to the silence, make loud, raucous noise,
learn to fall in directions of faith, however messy it may be.

TORI LANE

The First Nights of Autumn

Snap the spine of the paperback book,
flick the ash from the cigarette,
the sun will dip behind the moon
and give away the evening hours
with a cup of coffee, leather jacket,
and notes tucked into the margins.
The umbrella protects from the falling stars
and collects the smoky breath of poetry
exhaled on the air of change.
This is the time of transformation,
of the alteration of persons,
the reclamation of all beautiful things.
The night is impressionable,
scarred with the memories of its day,
tattooed with hopes for the dark of its mystery
and the dawn it so graciously precedes.
Grief is cradled in the words of her hand,
healing murmured in the lines of constellations,
sought, not always seen,
ever present in the darkened heavens
which dare the smoke to join it
in watching over the transitioning world.
The poet settles in to decipher the graffiti
of the smoke and stars sprayed overhead,
reading of history and God in the grey moon
and the white spaces of broken backed literature.

Happily Ever After

I've never really believed in happily ever after or dreams come true.
The whole dragon slaying, villain vanquishing,
kiss breaking the spell, riding off into the sunset –
even a good night sleep knowing all is well –
has always been the figment of minds
more imaginatively optimistic than mine.
I have had no such capacity for dreaming, hoping,
wishing, believing, fathoming in the remotest way –
until its recognizable reality bitch slapped me,
leaving a hand print on shrieking cheek,
knocking the wind of pessimistic sense out of me.
The unspoken, unacknowledged, unmuttered prayers,
the far too distant hopes tucked away as unarticulated secrets
demanded awareness in their unexpected fulfillment,
in the blessed answers to questions unasked.
The implausibilities entering into reality followed me
throughout the length of day in my shadow
and snuggled close in the newly restful sleep of night,
residing in the intimacy of inhaled and exhaled breath.
There has been no white knight or prince charming,
no spell breaking kiss,
and the sun still hangs high in the sky nowhere near its setting place,
but the epiphanic slap across the face forced sight to fall on the dragons slain in my wake,
on the empty spaces where now vanquished villains once stood,
on answered prayers that were never loosed to the air in admittance,
on the happy unfolding of ever after,
on the distressingly wondrous reality
that some dreams may actually come true.

To My Art

I think I could hate you,
or love you,
for the honesty of your existence.
You are hideously real, beautiful entirely.

You are the place of collision,
where everything exists in one damn fine mess –
the vocalized, common place, known pieces
and the quiet, unspoken,
noIdon'texistignoremeplease pieces as well.
All history, future, breath, knowledge,
fear, hope, faith, doubt and this moment
converge in the many spaces of you.

I often wonder what it'd be like
if I stripped you out of me,
peeled you from where you reside within my DNA.
I wouldn't know how to breathe deeply
or keep a steady heartbeat.
I would hate mornings.
My black notebook and pen
would stop following me everywhere I go.
I wouldn't beat up as many books,
drawing in their margins and folding their corners.
Coffee wouldn't taste as good
and I'd probably lose my proclivity for red wine.
The walls of my life would be bare,
no paint spatters or post-its,
doodles or sharpie made designs.
I wouldn't be me anymore without you.

I don't know how to like you,
only how to desperately need you,
waver between hating and loving you,
because you make me myself –
somehow hideously real, beautiful entirely.

About the Author

Tori Lane is a poet, dancer and visual artist living in Alexandria, Virginia. In 2010, Tori launched the Fusion Project, the focus of her artistic residency at Convergence, a Creative Community of Faith, where she began exploring the intersections of poetry and dance and started developing her skills as a performer. Tori continues to work at Convergence, where she performs and collaborates with other artists. *Falling Season* is Tori's first collection of published work.

Notes from the Author

Note about *Ella*

Ella was born with Epidermolysis Bullosa (EB), a rare genetic skin disease that causes the skin to be so fragile that the slightest friction can cause severe blistering, or cause the top layer of skin to come off completely. Today there is no cure. Currently, 1 out of every 50,000 live births in the United States are born with EB. For more information please visit www.debra.org.

Note about *Slowly, Slowly*, *Eggshells*, and *Khulumani*

H-E-A-R-T, Inc. was founded by Debbie Smith, a rape survivor who uses her experience in an effort to help others. Through "Victim to Victim Retreats", survivors are brought together and given the tools to develop a personal strategy for healing. Debbie can be reached at robanddeb@hughes.net or you can visit her web site at www.h-e-a-r-t.info.

CPSIA information can be obtained at www.ICGtesting.com
Printed in the USA
LVOW071534120413

328880LV00005B/604/P